Cursive Handwriting Practice Workbook

ALL RIGHTS RESERVED SPECIAL NEW EDUCATION PRESS
COPYRIGHT 2021

CAPITAL LETTERS IN CURSIVE

A B C D E F G

H I J K L M N

O P Q R S T U

V W X Y Z

NOTE: Trace over the dotted letters on the following pages then try writing the letters on your own in the blank space areas.

LOWERCASE LETERS IN CURSIVE

a b c d e f g h

i j k l m n o

p q r s t u v

w x y z

<u>NOTE</u>: On each right-hand side you will find plenty of space to practice handwritting.

Try writing these words one at a time.

Apple Apple Apple

Apple Apple Apple

apple apple apple

apple apple apple

First, let's practice writing a few sentences.

Apples taste good.

Apples taste good.

Apples are tasty.

Apples are tasty.

Try writing these words one at a time.

Bear Bear Bear Bear

Bear Bear Bear

bear bear bear bear

bear bear bear

Now, let's practice writing a few sentences.

Boys like to play.

Boys like to play.

Boys love toys.

Boys love toys.

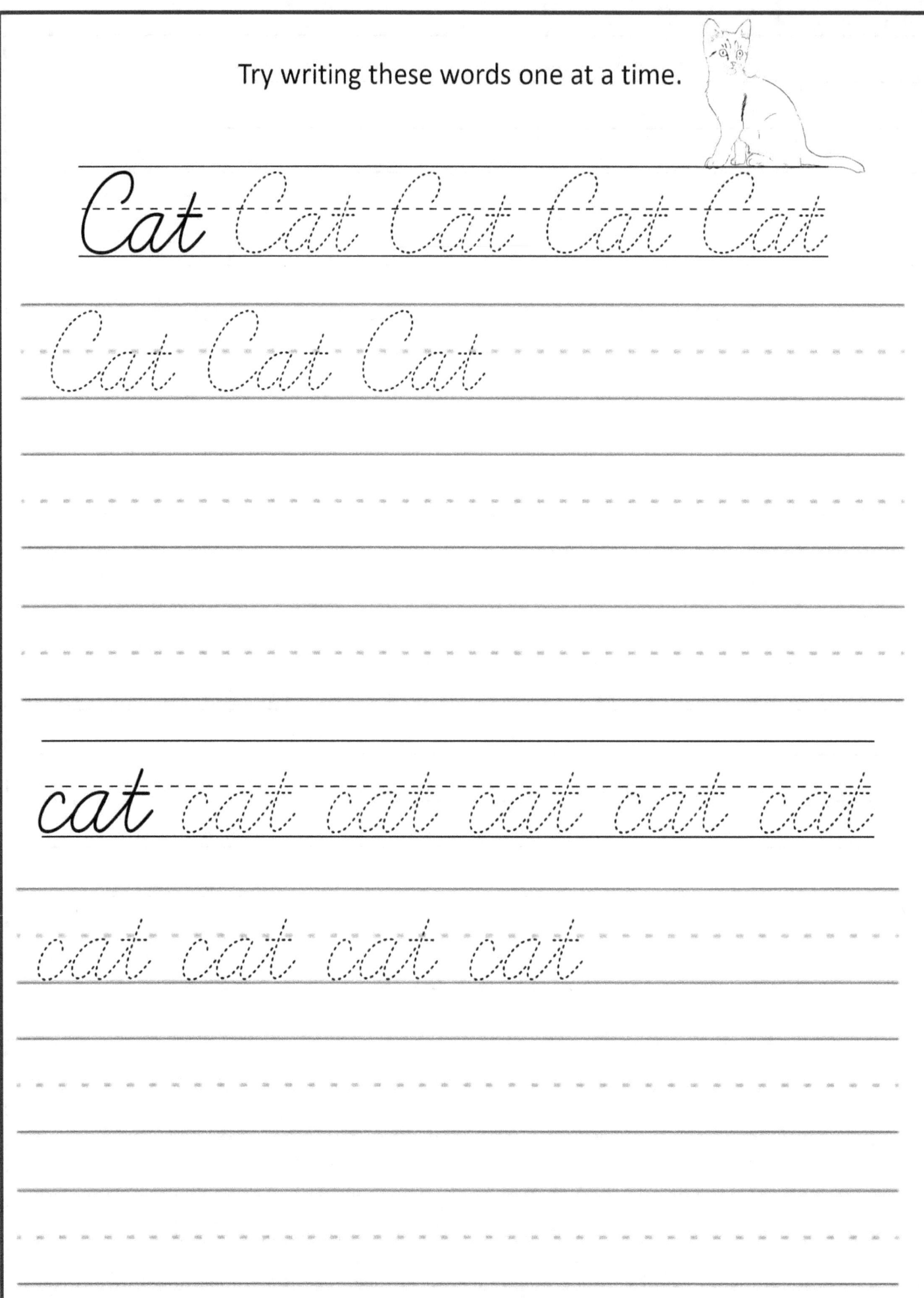

Try practice writing these sentences.

Cats meow.

Cats meow.

Cats purr.

Cats purr.

Try writing these words one at a time.

Dog Dog Dog Dog Dog

Dog Dog Dog

dog dog dog dog dog

dog dog dog

Now, let's practice writing these sentences.

Dogs bark.

Dogs bark.

Dogs dig.

Dogs dig.

Try writing these words one at a time.

Egg *Egg* *Egg* *Egg* *Egg*
Egg *Egg* *Egg*

egg *egg* *egg* *egg* *egg*
egg *egg* *egg*

First, let's practice writing a few sentences.

Eggs taste good.

Eggs taste good.

Eggs break.

Eggs break.

Try writing these words one at a time.

Fish Fish Fish Fish

Fish Fish Fish

fish fish fish fish fish

fish fish fish

Now, let's practice writing these sentences.

Football is fun.

Football is fun.

Fly a kite.

Fly a kite.

Try writing these words one at a time.

Goat Goat Goat Goat

Goat Goat Goat

goat goat goat goat

goat goat goat

Let's practice writing these sentences.

Go outside.

Go outside.

Giggle with me.

Giggle with me.

Try writing these words one at a time.

House House House

House House House

house house house

house house house

Try practice writing these sentences.

Hello friend.

Hello friend.

High in the sky.

High in the sky.

First, let's practice writing a few sentences.

Ice is cold.

Ice is cold.

Igloos are cool.

Igloos are cool.

Try writing these words one at a time.

Juice Juice Juice Juice

Juice Juice Juice

juice juice juice juice

juice juice juice

Let's practice writing these sentences.

Jelly is good.

Jelly is good.

Jam is better.

Jam is better.

Try writing these words one at a time.

Kite Kite Kite Kite Kite

Kite Kite Kite

kite kite kite kite kite

kite kite kite

Now let's practice writing these sentences.

Kings rule.

Kings rule.

Keys open doors.

Keys open doors.

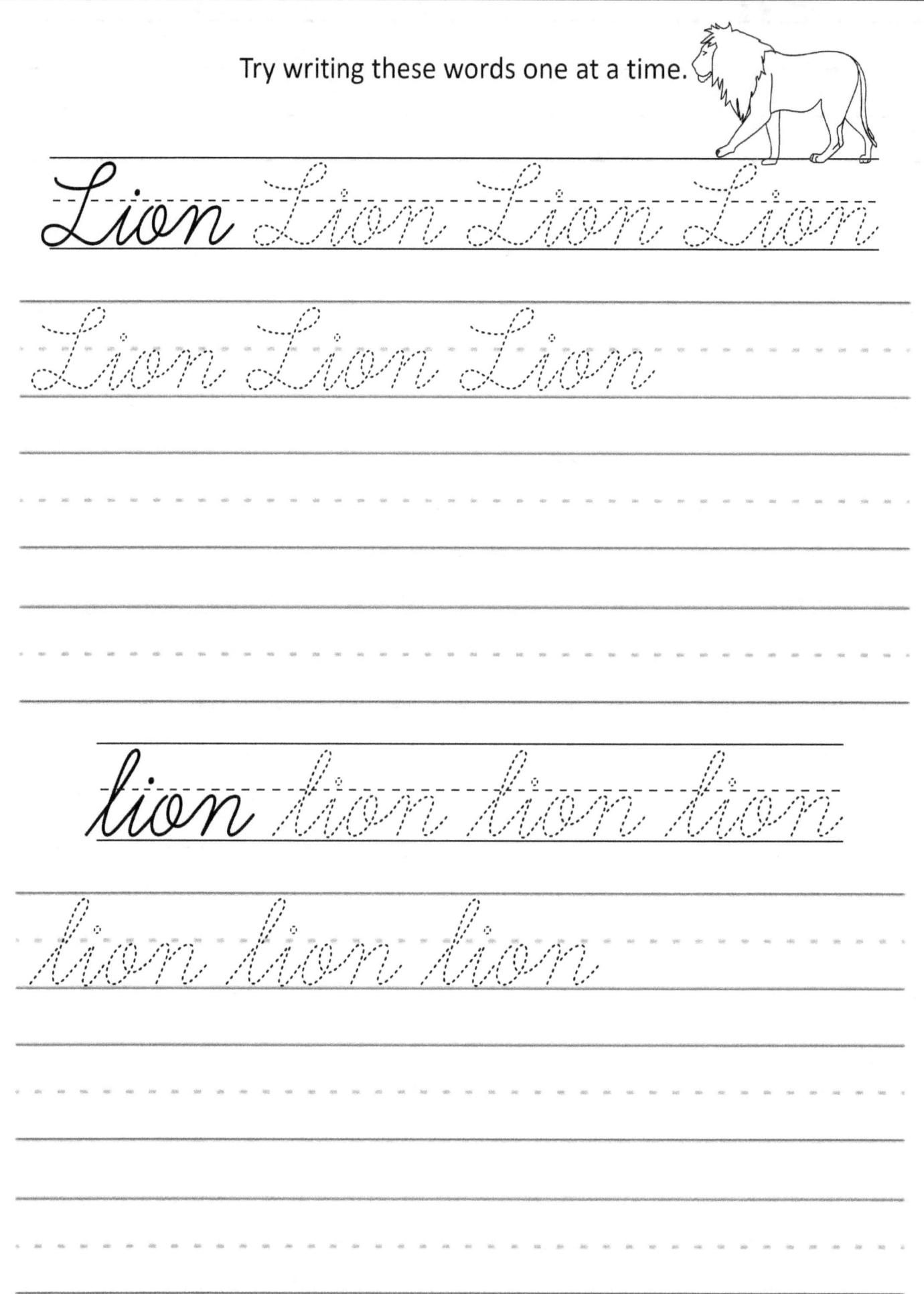

Try practice writing these sentences.

Leaves on trees.

Leaves on trees.

Lamps are bright.

Lamps are bright.

Try writing these words one at a time.

Mouse Mouse Mouse

Mouse Mouse Mouse

mouse mouse mouse

mouse mouse mouse

Let's practice writing these sentences.

Mice love cheese.

Mice love cheese.

Monsters are scary.

Monsters are scary.

Try writing these words one at a time.

Nest Nest Nest Nest

Nest Nest Nest

nest nest nest nest

nest nest nest

Next, let's write these sentences.

Noses itch.

Noses itch.

Nicely done.

Nicely done.

Try writing these words one at a time.

Owl Owl Owl Owl

Owl Owl Owl

owl owl owl owl owl

owl owl owl

Try practice writing these sentences.

Owls fly.

Owls fly.

Owls are birds.

Owls are birds.

Try writing these words one at a time.

Plane Plane Plane

Plane Plane Plane

plane plane plane

plane plane plane

Next, let's write these sentences.

Pandas are cute.

Pandas are cute.

Puppies are playful.

Puppies are playful.

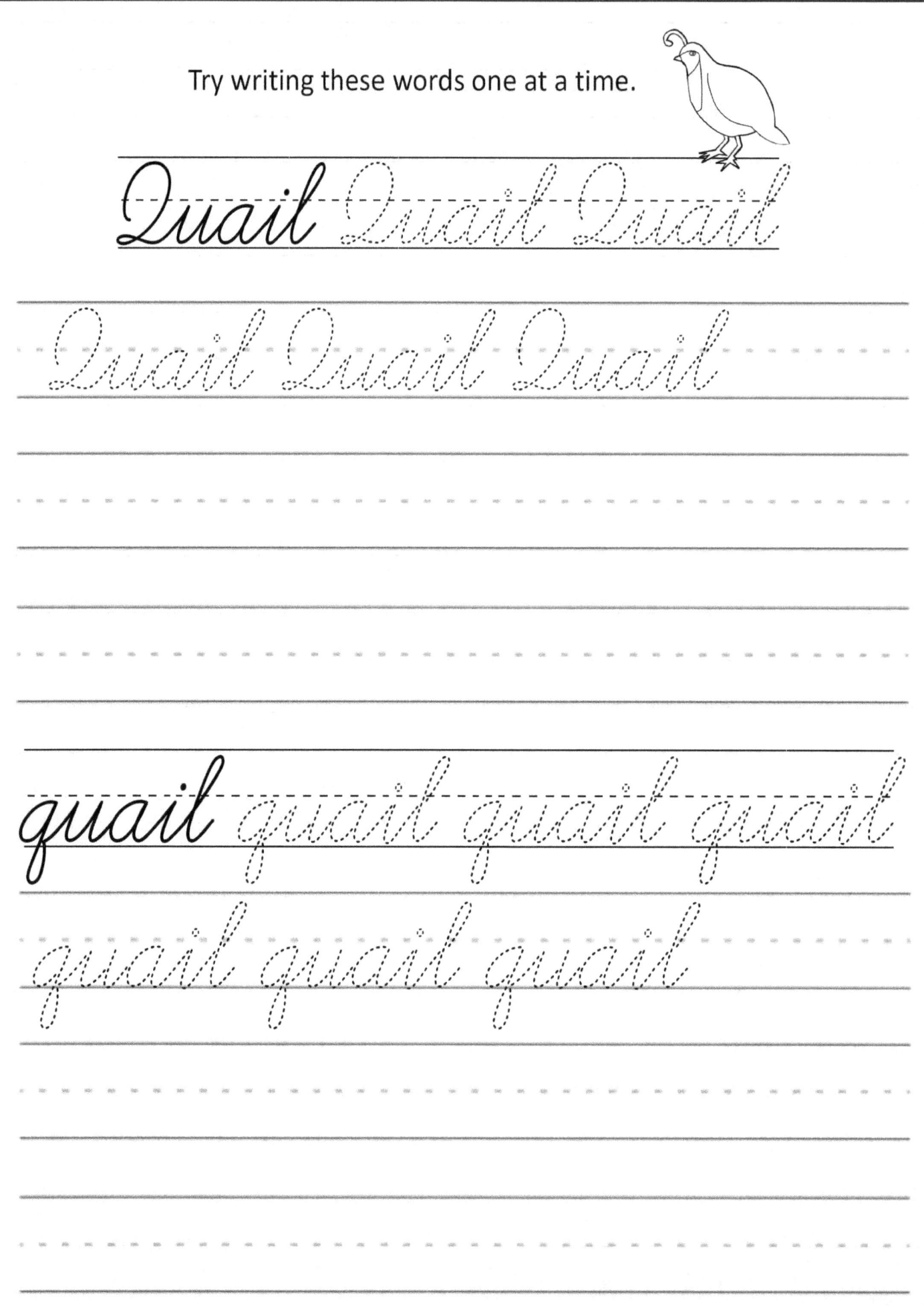

Try writing these sentences next.

Questions are good.

Questions are good.

Quails are birds.

Quails are birds.

Try writing these words one at a time.

Rose Rose Rose Rose

Rose Rose Rose

rose rose rose rose rose

rose rose rose

Try practice writing these sentences.

Roses smell good.

Roses smell good.

Red is pretty.

Red is pretty.

Try writing these words one at a time.

Sun Sun Sun Sun

Sun Sun Sun

sun sun sun sun sun

sun sun sun

First, let's practice writing a few sentences.

School is cool.

School is cool.

Sun shines bright.

Sun shines bright.

Try writing these words one at a time.

Tent Tent Tent Tent

Tent Tent Tent

tent tent tent tent

tent tent tent

Try writing these sentences next.

Toys are fun.

Toys are fun.

Tiny is cute.

Tiny is cute.

Try writing these words one at a time.

Up Up Up Up Up Up

Up Up Up

up up up up up up up

up up up

Now, let's practice writing these sentences.

Up there.

Up there.

Up and down.

Up and down.

Try writing these words one at a time.

Van Van Van Van

Van Van Van

van van van van

van van van

Try practice writing these sentences.

Vans are cool.

Vans are cool.

Violas sound nice.

Violas sound nice.

Try writing these words one at a time.

Watch Watch Watch

Watch Watch

watch watch watch

watch watch watch

First, let's practice writing a few sentences.

Watch me write.

Watch me write.

Write right.

Write right.

Try writing these words one at a time.

Xing Xing Xing Xing

Xing Xing

xing xing xing xing

xing xing xing

First, let's practice writing a few sentences.

Xenon is a gas.

Xenon is a gas.

X-rays work.

X-rays work.

Try writing these words one at a time.

Yam Yam Yam Yam

Yam Yam Yam

yam yam yam yam

yam yam yam

First, let's practice writing a few sentences.

Yams are tasty.

Yams are tasty.

Yummy food.

Yummy food.

Try writing these words one at a time.

Zebra Zebra Zebra

Zebra Zebra Zebra

zebra zebra zebra

zebra zebra zebra

First, let's practice writing a few sentences.

Zip zap zit.

Zip zap zit.

Zoom or boom.

Zoom or boom.

0

Zero

1   1 1 1 1 1 1 1 1
     1 1 1 1 1 1 1 1

1 1 1 1 1 1 1 1 1 1 1 1

One   One One One
      One One One

One One One One

2

Two

4

4 4 4 4 4 4 4

4 4 4 4 4 4 4

4 4 4 4 4 4 4 4 4

Four

Four Four Four

Four Four Four

Four Four Four Four

5

6

6 6 6 6 6 6 6
6 6 6 6 6 6 6

6 6 6 6 6 6 6 6 6 6

Six Six Six Six
     Six Six Six

Six Six Six Six Six

7

7 7 7 7 7 7 7

7 7 7 7 7 7 7

7 7 7 7 7 7 7 7

Seven   *Seven*   *Seven*

Seven   *Seven*

Seven Seven Seven

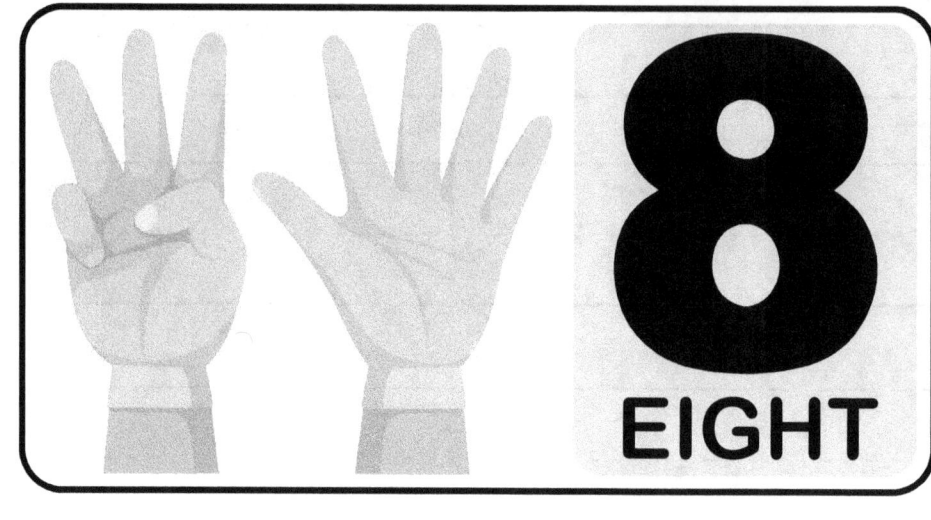

8   8 8 8 8 8 8 8

8 8 8 8 8 8 8

8 8 8 8 8 8 8 8 8 8

Eight   Eight   Eight

Eight   Eight

Eight   Eight   Eight

9

9 9 9 9 9 9 9 9

9 9 9 9 9 9 9 9

9 9 9 9 9 9 9 9 9 9 9

Nine

Nine Nine Nine

Nine Nine Nine

Nine Nine Nine Nine

I want to thank You for purchasing This Book. I would be very grateful for taking a moment and leaving feedback. It helps our small business grow and reach more people.

www.ingramcontent.com/pod-product-compliance
Lightning Source LLC
LaVergne TN
LVHW081547070526
838199LV00061B/4247